# One-Pot Cookbook: Family-Fri Soup, Casserole, Slow Cooker an for Busy People on a I

by **Vesela Tabakova**
Text copyright(c)2015 Vesela Tabakova

All rights reserved. No part of this publication may be reproduced, distributed, or transmitted in any form or by any means, including photocopying, recording, or other electronic or mechanical methods, without the prior written permission of the publisher, except in the case of brief quotations embodied in critical reviews and certain other noncommercial uses permitted by copyright law.

Although every precaution has been taken to verify the accuracy of the information contained herein, the author and publisher assume no responsibility for any errors or omissions. No liability is assumed for damages that may result from the use of information contained within.

# Table Of Contents

| | |
|---|---|
| Delicious One-Pot Meals to Please Everyone | 5 |
| Mediterranean Chicken Soup | 6 |
| Moroccan Chicken and Butternut Squash Soup | 7 |
| Chicken and Ricotta Meatball Soup | 9 |
| Bean, Chicken and Sausage Soup | 10 |
| Slow Cooker Chicken Broccoli Soup | 11 |
| Lentil and Ground Beef Soup | 12 |
| Italian Meatball Soup | 13 |
| Fish and Noodle Soup | 15 |
| Lentil, Barley and Kale Soup | 16 |
| Spinach and Mushroom Soup | 17 |
| Broccoli and Potato Soup | 18 |
| Moroccan Lentil Soup | 19 |
| Beetroot and Carrot Soup | 20 |
| Celery, Apple and Carrot Soup | 21 |
| Pumpkin and Bell Pepper Soup | 22 |
| Creamy Potato Soup | 23 |
| Wild Mushroom Soup | 24 |
| Spinach, Leek and Quinoa Soup | 25 |
| Vegetable Quinoa Soup | 26 |
| Slow Cooker Tuscan-style Soup | 27 |
| Lamb and Potato Casserole | 28 |
| Mediterranean Baked Fish | 29 |
| Mediterranean Chicken Casserole | 30 |
| Chicken and Potato Casserole | 31 |
| Mediterranean Chicken Drumstick Casserole | 32 |
| Greek Chicken Casserole | 33 |
| Chicken with Almonds and Prunes | 34 |
| Chicken and Rice Casserole | 35 |
| Easy Chicken Paella | 36 |
| Chicken and Artichoke Rice | 37 |
| Easy Chicken Parmigiana | 38 |
| One-Pot Chicken Dijonnaise | 39 |
| Sweet and Sour Sicilian Chicken | 40 |
| Lemon Rosemary Chicken | 41 |

| | |
|---|---|
| Chicken and Bacon Frittata | 42 |
| Chicken and Zucchini Frittata | 43 |
| Beef and Pumpkin Stew | 44 |
| Beef and Onion Stew | 45 |
| Beef Stew with Green Peas | 46 |
| Beef and Spinach Stew | 47 |
| Mediterranean Beef Casserole | 48 |
| Beef and Broccoli Stir Fry | 49 |
| Beef Stew with Quince | 50 |
| Spanish Beef Stew | 52 |
| Ground Beef and Chickpea Casserole | 53 |
| Spinach with Ground Beef | 54 |
| Delicious One-Pot Ground Beef Pasta | 55 |
| Sausage and Beans | 56 |
| Mediterranean Pork Casserole | 57 |
| Pork and Rice Casserole | 58 |
| Pork Roast and Cabbage | 59 |
| Orange Pork Chops | 60 |
| Pork and Mushroom Crock Pot | 61 |
| Bacon and Mushroom Frittata | 62 |
| Brussels Sprouts with Bacon and Onion | 63 |
| Zucchini Bake | 64 |
| Baked Cauliflower | 65 |
| Potato and Zucchini Bake | 66 |
| Artichoke and Onion Frittata | 67 |
| Green Pea and Mushroom Stew | 68 |
| Tomato and Leek Stew | 69 |
| Potato and Leek Stew | 70 |
| Baked Bean and Rice Casserole | 71 |
| Creamy Green Pea and Rice Casserole | 72 |
| Zucchini and Rice Stew | 73 |
| Spinach with Rice | 74 |
| Eggplant Casserole | 75 |
| Eggplant and Chickpea Casserole | 76 |
| Ratatouille | 77 |
| Rice Stuffed Bell Peppers | 78 |

| | |
|---|---|
| Green Bean and Potato Stew | 79 |
| Cabbage and Rice Stew | 80 |
| Rice with Leeks and Olives | 81 |
| Rice and Tomato Stew | 82 |
| Okra and Tomato Casserole | 83 |
| Spinach with Eggs | 84 |
| Mish-Mash | 85 |
| Vegetable Quinoa Pilaf | 86 |
| Spinach, Lentil and Quinoa Casserole | 87 |
| Rich Vegetable One-Pot Pasta | 88 |
| One-Pot Broccoli Pasta | 89 |
| FREE BONUS RECIPES: 10 Ridiculously Easy Jam and Jelly Recipes Anyone Can Make | 90 |
| A Different Strawberry Jam | 91 |
| Raspberry Jam | 92 |
| Raspberry-Peach Jam | 93 |
| Blueberry Jam | 94 |
| Triple Berry Jam | 95 |
| Red Currant Jelly | 96 |
| White Cherry Jam | 97 |
| Cherry Jam | 98 |
| Oven Baked Ripe Fig Jam | 99 |
| Quince Jam | 100 |
| About the Author | 101 |

## Delicious One-Pot Meals to Please Everyone

In a world where food is full of frightening artificial additives and flavorings, there is one simple and easy way to adopt a healthier lifestyle - the more unprocessed and real food you eat, the better.

While it may look and sound difficult to cook real food at home you will soon realize you can throw together a healthy one-pot family dinner in the same amount of time you'd need to order a takeout. Homemade one-pot cooking is the easiest and stress-free way of preparing fast, yet healthy dinners for the family. When time is short and all you want is to spend more time with your family,one-pot soups, stews, casseroles and chillis are just the thing to cook. All you need to do is cut up your favorite vegetables, meats and legumes, throw them together with your favorite spices in a single pot, skillet or slow cooker and you will have a quick weeknight supper or a delicious weekend dinner - it doesn't get any easier than that!

At the end of a busy day one-pot cooking is just what you need to prepare delicious family dinners which are sure to please everyone at the table and to become all time favorites.

# Mediterranean Chicken Soup

**Serves 5-6**

**Ingredients:**

1.5 lb chicken breasts

3-4 carrots, chopped

1 celery rib, chopped

1 red onion, chopped

1/3 cup rice, rinsed

8 cups water

10 black olives, pitted and halved

1/2 tsp salt

ground black pepper, to taste

lemon juice, to serve

1/2 cup fresh parsley or coriander, finely cut, to serve

**Directions:**

Place chicken breasts in a soup pot. Add in onion, carrots, celery, salt, pepper and water. Stir well and bring to a boil.

Add in rice and olives. Stir and reduce heat. Simmer for 30-40 minutes.

Remove chicken from the pot and let it cool. Shred it and return it back to the pot.

Serve soup with lemon juice and sprinkled with fresh parsley or coriander.

# Moroccan Chicken and Butternut Squash Soup

**Serves 5-6**

**Ingredients:**

3 skinless, boneless chicken thighs (about 14 oz), cut into bite-sized pieces

1 large onion, chopped

1 zucchini, quartered lengthwise and sliced into 1/2-inch pieces

3 cups peeled butternut squash, cut in 1/2-inch pieces

2 tbsp tomato paste

4 cups chicken broth

1/3 cup uncooked couscous

3 tbsp olive oil

1/2 tsp ground cumin

1/4 tsp cinnamon

1 tsp paprika

2 tbsp fresh basil leaves, chopped

1 tbsp grated orange rind

**Directions:**

Heat a soup pot over medium heat. Gently sauté onion, stirring occasionally. Add in chicken pieces and cook for 3-4 minutes until chicken is brown on all sides.

Add cumin, cinnamon and paprika and stir well. Add butternut squash and tomato paste; stir again.

Add chicken broth and bring to a boil then reduce heat and simmer for ten minutes.

Stir in couscous, salt and zucchini pieces and cook until squash is tender. Remove pot from heat. Season with salt and pepper to taste.

Stir in chopped basil and orange rind and serve.

## Chicken and Ricotta Meatball Soup

**Serves 4-5**

**Ingredients:**

1 lb ground chicken meat

1 egg, lightly whisked

1 cup whole milk Ricotta

1 cup grated Parmesan cheese

1-2 tbsp flour

1/2 onion, chopped

4 cups chicken broth

2 cups baby spinach

1/2 tsp dried oregano

3 tbsp olive oil

½ tsp black pepper

**Directions:**

Place ground chicken, Ricotta, Parmesan, egg and black pepper in a bowl. Combine well with hands and roll teaspoonfuls of the mixture into balls. Roll each meatball in the flour then set aside on a large plate.

In a deep soup pot, heat olive oil and gently sauté onion until transparent. Add in oregano and chicken broth and bring to a boil. Add meatballs, reduce heat, and simmer, uncovered, for 15 minutes.

Add baby spinach leaves and simmer for 2 more minutes until it wilts.

# Bean, Chicken and Sausage Soup

**Serves 4-5**

**Ingredients:**

10.5 oz Italian sausage

2 bacon strips, diced

1 cup chicken, cooked and diced

1 cup canned kidney beans, rinsed and drained

1 onion, chopped

2 garlic cloves, crushed

4 cups water

1 cup canned tomatoes, diced, undrained

1 bay leaf

1 tsp dried thyme

1 tsp savory

1/2 tsp dried basil

salt and pepper, to taste

**Directions:**

In a deep soup pot, cook the sausage, onion and bacon over medium heat until the sausage is no longer pink. Drain off the fat. Add in the garlic and cook for a minute until just fragrant.

Add water, tomatoes and seasonings and bring to a boil. Cover, reduce heat, and simmer for 30 minutes. Add chicken and beans. Simmer for five minutes and serve.

# Slow Cooker Chicken Broccoli Soup

**Serves 6-7**

**Ingredients:**

2 lb boneless chicken thighs, cut in bite sized pieces

1 small onion, chopped

1 fresh garlic clove

6-7 fresh or frozen broccoli florets

4 cups chicken broth

2 potatoes, peeled and cubed

3 tbsp olive oil

1 tsp garlic powder

1 tsp dried oregano

1 tsp salt

black pepper, to taste

12 oz cheddar cheese, to serve

**Directions:**

In a skillet, sauté onion and garlic with olive oil until onion is translucent.

Season the chicken well with salt, black pepper, garlic powder and oregano. Place it in slow cooker with the onion mixture and all remaining ingredients.

Cover and cook on low for 8-10 hours or on high for 4-5 hours. Serve topped with cheddar cheese.

# Lentil and Ground Beef Soup

**Serves 4-5**

**Ingredients:**

1 lb ground beef

1 cup brown lentils

2 carrots, chopped

1 onion, chopped

1 potato, peeled and diced

4 garlic cloves, chopped

2 tomatoes, grated or pureed

5 cups water

1 tsp summer savory

1 tsp paprika

2 tbsp olive oil

1 tsp salt

ground black pepper, to taste

**Directions:**

Heat olive oil in a large soup pot. Brown the ground beef, breaking it up with a spoon. Add in paprika and garlic and stir. Add lentils, remaining vegetables, water and spice.

Bring the soup to a boil. Reduce heat to low and simmer, covered, for about an hour, or until the lentils are tender. Stir occasionally.

# Italian Meatball Soup

**Serves 4-5**

**Ingredients:**

1 lb ground beef

1 small onion, grated

1 onion, chopped

2 garlic cloves, crushed

1 zucchini, diced

½ cup green beans, trimmed, halved

½ cup breadcrumbs

3-4 basil leaves, finely chopped

1/3 cup Parmesan cheese, grated

1 egg, lightly beaten

2 cups tomato sauce

3 cups water

½ cup small pasta

2 tbsp olive oil

salt and black pepper, to taste

**Directions:**

Combine the ground beef with grated onion, garlic, breadcrumbs, basil, Parmesan and an egg in a large bowl. Season with salt and pepper. Mix well with hands and roll tablespoonfuls of the mixture into balls. Place on a plate.

Heat olive oil into a large deep soup pot and sauté onion and garlic until transparent. Add in tomato sauce and water, and bring to a boil over high heat.

Add the meatballs, reduce heat to medium-low and simmer, uncovered, for 15 minutes. Add in pasta and cook for 5 more minutes. Add the zucchini and green beans.

Cook until pasta and vegetables are tender. Serve sprinkled with Parmesan cheese.

# Fish and Noodle Soup

**Serves 4-5**

**Ingredients:**

14 oz firm white fish, cut into strips

2 carrots, cut into ribbons

1 zucchini, cut into thin ribbons

7 oz white button mushrooms, sliced

1 celery rib, finely cut

1 cup baby spinach

7 oz fresh noodles

3 cups chicken broth

2 cups water

2 tbsp soy sauce

1/2 tsp ground ginger

black pepper, to taste

**Directions:**

Place chicken broth, water and soy sauce in a large saucepan. Bring to a boil and add in carrots, celery, zucchini, mushrooms, ginger and noodles.

Cook, partially covered, for 3-4 minutes then add in fish and simmer for 3 minutes or until the fish is cooked through. Add baby spinach and simmer, stirring, for a minute, or until it wilts.

Season with black pepper and serve.

# Lentil, Barley and Kale Soup

**Serves 4**

**Ingredients:**

2 medium leeks, chopped

2 garlic cloves, chopped

2 bay leaves

1 can tomatoes, diced and undrained

1/2 cup red lentils

1/2 cup barley

1 bunch kale, coarsely chopped

4 cups vegetable broth

3 tbsp olive oil

1 tbsp paprika

½ tsp cumin

**Directions:**

Heat olive oil in a large saucepan over medium-high heat and sauté leeks and garlic until fragrant. Add in cumin, paprika, tomatoes, lentils, barley and vegetable broth. Season with salt and pepper.

Cover, and bring to a boil then reduce heat and simmer for 40 minutes or until barley is tender. Add in kale and let it simmer for a few minutes more until it wilts.

# Spinach and Mushroom Soup

**Serves 4-5**

**Ingredients:**

1 small onion, finely cut

1 small carrot, chopped

1 small zucchini, peeled and diced

1 medium potato, peeled and diced

6-7 white button mushrooms, chopped

2 cups chopped fresh spinach

4 cups vegetable broth or water

4 tbsp olive oil

salt and black pepper, to taste

**Directions:**

Heat olive oil in a large soup pot over medium heat. Add in potato, onion and mushroom and cook until vegetables are soft but not mushy.

Add chopped fresh spinach, zucchini and vegetable broth and simmer for about 15 minutes. Season to taste with salt and pepper and serve.

# Broccoli and Potato Soup

**Serves 4-5**

**Ingredients:**

1 lb broccoli, cut into florets

2 potatoes, peeled and chopped

1 onion, chopped

3 garlic cloves, crushed

4 cups water

2 tbsp olive oil

¼ tsp ground nutmeg

**Directions:**

Heat oil in a large saucepan over medium-high heat. Add in onion and garlic and sauté, stirring, for 3 minutes or until soft.

Add in broccoli, potato and 4 cups of cold water. Cover, bring to a boil, reduce heat and simmer, stirring, for 10-15 minutes, or until potatoes are tender.

Remove from heat and blend until smooth. Return to saucepan and cook until heated through. Season with nutmeg and black pepper and serve.

# Moroccan Lentil Soup

**Serves 6-7**

**Ingredients:**

1 cup red lentils

1 cup canned chickpeas, drained

1 onion, chopped

2 cloves garlic, minced

1 cup canned tomatoes, chopped

1 cup canned white beans, drained

3 carrots, diced

1 celery rib, diced

5 cups water

3 tbsp olive oil

1 tsp ginger, grated

1 tsp ground cardamom

1/2 tsp cumin

**Directions:**

In a large soup pot, sauté onions, garlic and ginger in olive oil for about 5 minutes. Add in water, lentils, chickpeas, white beans, tomatoes, carrots, celery, cardamom and cumin.

Bring to a boil for a few minutes then lower heat and simmer for half an hour or longer until the lentils are tender. Puree half the soup in a food processor or blender.

Return the pureed soup to the pot, stir and serve.

# Beetroot and Carrot Soup

**Serves 5-6**

**Ingredients:**

4 beets, washed and peeled

2 carrots, peeled, chopped

2 potatoes, peeled, chopped

1 small onion, chopped

2 cups vegetable broth

2 cups water

3 tbsp olive oil

1 cup finely cut green onions, to serve

**Directions:**

Heat olive oil in a deep saucepan over medium-high heat and sauté the onion and carrot until tender. Add in beets, potatoes, broth and water.

Bring to the boil then reduce heat and simmer, partially covered, for 30 minutes, or until beets are tender.

Set aside to cool then blend in batches until smooth. Return soup to saucepan and cook, stirring, for 4-5 minutes, or until heated through.

Season with salt and pepper and serve sprinkled with green onions.

# Celery, Apple and Carrot Soup

**Serves 4**

**Ingredients:**

2 celery ribs, chopped

1 large apple, chopped

1/2 small onion, chopped

3 carrots, chopped

2 garlic cloves, crushed

4 cups vegetable broth

3 tbsp olive oil

1 tsp ground ginger

salt and black pepper, to taste

**Directions:**

In a deep saucepan, heat olive oil over medium-high heat and sauté onion, garlic, celery and carrots for 3-4 minutes, stirring. Add in ginger, apple and vegetable broth.

Bring to a boil then reduce heat and simmer, covered, for 10 minutes. Blend until smooth and return to the pot. Cook over medium-high heat until heated through. Season with salt and pepper to taste and serve.

# Pumpkin and Bell Pepper Soup

**Serves 4**

**Ingredients:**

1 medium leek, chopped

9 oz pumpkin, peeled, deseeded, cut into small cubes

1 red bell pepper, cut into small pieces

1 can tomatoes, undrained, crushed

3 cups vegetable broth

1/2 tsp cumin

salt and black pepper, to taste

**Directions:**

Heat the olive oil in a medium saucepan and sauté the leek for 4-5 minutes. Add in the pumpkin and bell pepper and cook, stirring, for 5 minutes. Add tomatoes, broth, and cumin and bring to a boil.

Cover, reduce heat to low, and simmer, stirring occasionally, for 30 minutes or until vegetables are soft. Season with salt and pepper and leave aside to cool.

Blend in batches and reheat to serve.

# Creamy Potato Soup

**Serves 6-7**

**Ingredients:**

4-5 medium potatoes, peeled and diced

2 carrots, chopped

1 zucchini, chopped

1 celery rib, chopped

5 cups water

3 tbsp olive oil

½ tsp dried rosemary

salt and black pepper, to taste

1/2 cup fresh parsley, finely cut

**Directions:**

In a deep soup pot, heat olive oil over medium heat and sauté the vegetables and rosemary for 2-3 minutes. Add in 4 cups of water and bring the soup to a boil then lower heat and simmer until all the vegetables are tender.

Blend soup in a blender until smooth. Serve warm, seasoned with black pepper and fresh parsley sprinkled over each serving.

# Wild Mushroom Soup

**Serves 4**

**Ingredients:**

1 lb mixed wild mushrooms

1 onion, chopped

2 garlic cloves, crushed

1 tsp dried thyme

3 cups vegetable broth

3 tbsp olive oil

salt and pepper, to taste

**Directions:**

Sauté onions and garlic in a large soup pot until transparent. Add thyme and mushrooms. Stir, and cook for 10 minutes, then add vegetable broth and simmer for another 10-20 minutes.

Blend, season and serve.

# Spinach, Leek and Quinoa Soup

**Serves 4-5**

**Ingredients:**

½ cup quinoa, very well washed

2 leeks halved lengthwise and sliced

1 onion, chopped

2 garlic cloves, chopped

1 can diced tomatoes, (15 oz), undrained

2 cups fresh spinach, cut

4 cups vegetable broth

2 tbsp olive oil

salt and pepper, to taste

**Directions:**

Heat olive oil in a large soup pot over medium heat and sauté onion for 2 minutes, stirring. Add in leeks and cook for another 2-3 minutes. Stir in garlic, salt and black pepper to taste. Add the vegetable broth, canned tomatoes and quinoa.

Bring to a boil then reduce heat and simmer for 10 minutes. Stir in spinach and cook for another 5 minutes.

# Vegetable Quinoa Soup

**Serves 6**

**Ingredients:**

½ cup quinoa

1/2 onion, chopped

1 potato, peeled and diced

1 carrot, diced

1 red bell pepper, chopped

2 tomatoes, chopped

1 small zucchini, peeled and diced

4 cups water

1 tsp dried oregano

3-4 tbsp olive oil

black pepper, to taste

2 tbsp fresh lemon juice

**Directions:**

Rinse quinoa very well in a fine mesh strainer under running water; set aside to drain.

Heat olive oil in a large soup pot and gently sauté the onion and carrot for 2-3 minutes, stirring every now and then. Add in potato, bell pepper, tomatoes, oregano and water.

Stir to combine, cover, and bring to a boil then lower heat and simmer for 10 minutes.

Add in quinoa and zucchini; cover and simmer for 15 minutes or until the vegetables are tender. Add in lemon juice; stir to combine and serve.

# Slow Cooker Tuscan-style Soup

**Serves 5-6**

**Ingredients:**

1 lb potatoes, peeled and cubed

1 small onion, chopped

1 can mixed beans, drained

1 carrot, chopped

2 garlic cloves, chopped

4 cups chicken broth

1 cups chopped kale

3 tbsp olive oil

1 bay leaf

salt and pepper, to taste

Parmesan cheese, to serve

**Directions:**

Heat oil in a skillet over medium heat and sauté the onion, carrot and garlic, stirring, for 2-3 minutes or until soft.

Combine all ingredients except the kale into the slow cooker. Season with salt and pepper to taste.

Cook on high for 4 hours or low for 6-7 hours. Add in kale about 30 minutes before soup is finished cooking. Serve sprinkled with Parmesan cheese.

# Lamb and Potato Casserole

**Serves 6**

**Ingredients:**

1 1/2 pounds shoulder lamb chops

12 small new potatoes, peeled, whole

3 onions, sliced

2 carrots, sliced

2 tbsp olive oil

2 tsp dried parsley

2 tsp dried mint

1/2 tsp pepper

1/2 tsp salt

**Directions:**

Place lamb chops into a greased casserole dish. Cover them with sliced onion, carrots, parsley, salt and pepper. Arrange new potatoes on and around the meat. Add enough cold water to fill the dish halfway and season with mint, salt and pepper.

Cover and bake, for 60 minutes, in a preheated to 350 F oven.

# Mediterranean Baked Fish

**Serves 4**

**Ingredients:**

1 ½ flounder or sole fillets

3 tomatoes, chopped

1/2 onion, chopped

2 cloves garlic, chopped

1/3 cup white wine

20 black olives, pitted and chopped

1 tbsp capers

3 tbsp Parmesan cheese

3 tbsp olive oil

1 tbsp fresh lemon juice

1 tsp dried oregano

4 leaves fresh basil, chopped

**Directions:**

Heat olive oil in an oven-proof casserole dish and sauté onion until translucent, 2-3 minutes. Add in garlic, oregano, tomatoes, wine, olives, capers, lemon juice and the chopped basil.

Stir in Parmesan cheese and arrange fish in this sauce.

Bake for 30 minutes in a preheated to 350 F oven, until fish is easily flaked with a fork.

# Mediterranean Chicken Casserole

**Serves 4**

**Ingredients:**

4-5 chicken breast halves

1 large onion, sliced

1 red bell pepper, thinly sliced

2 cups tomato pasta sauce

1/2 cup black olives, pitted

1/2 green olives, pitted

1/3 cup Parmesan cheese

1/2 cup chopped parsley

3 tbsp olive oil

salt and black pepper, to taste

**Directions:**

Heat olive oil in a large, deep saucepan over medium-high heat. Cook chicken breasts, turning, for 4 to 5 minutes or until golden.

Add in onion and bell pepper, pasta sauce and olives. Season with salt and pepper.

Cover, and simmer 30-35 minutes, stirring halfway through. Sprinkle with Parmesan cheese and parsley and serve.

# Chicken and Potato Casserole

**Serves 4**

**Ingredients:**

4 skinless, boneless chicken breast halves

12 oz new potatoes

1 onion, sliced

2 carrots, cut

1 red bell pepper, halved, deseeded, cut

1 zucchini, peeled and cut

4 garlic cloves, thinly sliced

1 cup water

3 tbsp olive oil

1 tsp dried oregano

salt and pepper, to taste

**Directions:**

Heat olive oil in an oven-proof casserole dish and brown the chicken breasts.

Peel and cut all vegetables and add them on and around the chicken.

Season with salt and pepper, to taste. Sprinkle with oregano, add in water, and bake, uncovered, at 350 F for 45 minutes.

# Mediterranean Chicken Drumstick Casserole

**Serves 4**

*Ingredients*:

8 chicken drumsticks

1 leek, trimmed, thinly sliced

2 garlic cloves, crushed

1 cup tomatoes, diced

1 cup black olives, pitted

1 cup canned chickpeas, drained and rinsed

2 tbsp olive oil

1 tsp dried rosemary

salt and black pepper, to taste

**Directions:**

Heat olive oil in an oven-proof casserole dish and brown the chicken drumsticks. Add in leek, garlic, tomatoes, chickpeas, olives and rosemary.

Cover, and bake in a preheated to 350 F oven, for 40 minutes, or until chicken is tender. Season with salt and pepper to taste.

# Greek Chicken Casserole

**Serves 5-6**

**Ingredients:**

4-5 skinless, boneless chicken breast halves or 8 tights

2 lb potatoes, peeled and cubed

1/2 lb green beans, trimmed and cut in 1 inch pieces

1 large onion, chopped

2 cups diced, canned tomatoes, undrained

5 cloves garlic, minced

1/4 cup water

1 cup feta cheese, crumbled

salt and black pepper, to taste

**Directions:**

Heat olive oil in an oven-proof casserole dish and brown the chicken. Add in onion, thyme, black pepper and garlic, and sauté for a minute, stirring.

Add in potatoes, green beans, water and tomatoes, season with salt and pepper to taste, and top with crumbled feta.

Cover and bake, in a preheated to 350 F oven, for 40 minutes.

# Chicken with Almonds and Prunes

**Serves 4**

**Ingredients:**

1.5 lb chicken thigh fillets

1/3 cup fresh orange juice

2 tbsp honey

1/3 cup white wine

1/2 cup pitted prunes

2 tbsp blanched almonds

2 tbsp raisins or sultanas

1 tsp ground cinnamon

salt and black pepper, to taste

1/2 cup fresh parsley leaves, chopped, to serve

**Directions:**

Heat olive oil in a large saucepan over medium heat. Cook the chicken pieces until nicely browned, 3-4 minutes each side. Add in orange juice, wine, honey, prunes, almonds, raisins and cinnamon.

Bring to a boil, reduce heat to medium, and simmer 35 minutes, or until chicken is just tender.

Season to taste with salt and pepper, sprinkle with parsley, and serve.

# Chicken and Rice Casserole

**Serves 6**

**Ingredients:**

1 chicken 2-3 lbs, cut into serving pieces, or 2 lbs chicken thighs or breasts

1 medium onion, chopped

1 carrot, chopped

1 garlic clove, minced

1 1/2 cups white rice

2 cups chicken broth

2 cups water

1 cup of diced fresh or cooked tomatoes, drained

3 tbsp olive oil

1 tsp supper savory

1 tsp salt

black pepper, to taste

**Directions:**

Heat olive oil in an oven-proof casserole dish on medium-high heat. Cook chicken pieces for a few minutes on each side, enough to seal them.

Add in onions, garlic, carrot and rice and cook, stirring for 1-2 minutes, until the rice becomes transparent.

Stir in chicken broth, water and tomatoes, season with salt and pepper to taste, and bake in a preheated to 350 F oven for 45 minutes until the rice and chicken are done.

# Easy Chicken Paella

**Serves 4**

**Ingredients:**

4 chicken thigh fillets, trimmed and cut into pieces

1 red onion, chopped

1 large red bell pepper, chopped

1 1/2 cups rice

2 cups chicken broth

1/2 cup frozen peas, thawed

1/2 cup parsley leaves, finely cut

1 tbsp paprika

1/2 tsp saffron

2 tbsp boiling water

2 tbsp olive oil

lemon wedges, to serve

**Directions:**

Place saffron in a small cup and add two tablespoons of boiling water. Set aside for 5 minutes.

Heat olive oil in a large saucepan over high heat and cook chicken 3-4 minutes or until golden. Add in onion and cook some more. Add paprika, red pepper and rice and stir to combine. Add saffron mixture, green peas and chicken broth then bring to a boil.

Reduce heat to low and simmer, covered, stirring from time to time, for 10-15 minutes, or until rice is just tender.

Serve with lemon wedges.

# Chicken and Artichoke Rice

**Serves 4**

**Ingredients:**

3 skinless chicken breasts, cut into strips

2 leeks, white parts only, chopped

7-8 canned artichoke hearts, quartered

2 garlic cloves, crushed

2/3 cup rice

2 cups chicken broth

2 tbsp olive oil

1 tsp lemon rind

7-8 fresh basil leaves, chopped

1 bay leaf

juice of 1 lemon

**Directions:**

Heat the oil in a large saucepan over low heat. Gently sauté the leeks, bay leaf and garlic for about 3-4 minutes, stirring occasionally. Add in the lemon rind and the chicken breasts and cook, stirring, for 5-6 minutes.

Add rice, stir, and add chicken broth and half the lemon juice.

Bring to the boil then reduce heat, cover, and cook for 10 minutes.

Set aside, covered, for 5 minutes then stir in the chopped basil, artichoke hearts and remaining lemon juice.

# Easy Chicken Parmigiana

**Serves 4**

**Ingredients:**

4 chicken breast fillets

1 eggplant, peeled and sliced lengthwise

1 can tomatoes, diced

9 oz mozzarella cheese, sliced

2 tbsp olive oil

**Directions:**

In an oven-proof casserole, heat olive oil and brown the chicken pieces.

Place eggplant over the chicken and add in tomatoes. Top with mozzarella slices and bake in a preheated to 350 F for 20 minutes or until cheese is golden.

## One-Pot Chicken Dijonnaise

**Serves 4**

**Ingredients:**

4 chicken breasts with skin

1 onion, sliced

5-6 white button mushrooms, sliced

2 garlic cloves, crushed

1 tbsp flour

1/3 cup Dijon mustard

1/3 cup mayonnaise

1/3 cup dry white wine

1/3 cup chicken broth

1/2 cup sour cream

2 tbsp olive oil

2 tbsp finely chopped tarragon

**Directions:**

Heat oil in an oven-proof casserole over medium heat. Cook chicken in batches for 2-3 minutes each side until golden. Add onion and sauté for 3 more minutes or until soft.

Stir in the mushrooms and garlic and cook, stirring, for a further minute. Add in flour and stir to combine. Add wine, mayonnaise, Dijon mustard, chicken broth and tarragon and combine well.

Cover with a lid or foil and bake in a preheated to 380 F oven for 10-15 minutes or until chicken is cooked through and the liquid has evaporated. Add in sour cream, salt and black pepper to taste and heat through.

# Sweet and Sour Sicilian Chicken

**Serves 4**

**Ingredients:**

4 chicken thigh fillets

1 large red onion, sliced

3 garlic cloves, chopped

2 tbsp flour

1/3 cup dry white wine

1 cup chicken broth

1/2 cup green olives

2 tbsp olive oil

2 bay leaves

1 tbsp fresh oregano leaves

2 tbsp brown sugar or honey

2 tbsp red wine vinegar

salt and black pepper, to taste

**Directions:**

Combine the flour with salt and black pepper and coat well all chicken pieces. Heat oil in oven-proof casserole and cook the chicken in batches, for 1-2 minutes each side, or until golden.

Add in onion, garlic, and wine and cook, stirring for 1 more minute. Add the chicken broth, olives, bay leaves, oregano, sugar and vinegar and bake, in a preheated to 380 F oven, for 20 minutes, or until the chicken is cooked through.

# Lemon Rosemary Chicken

**Serves 4**

**Ingredients:**

4 boneless skinless chicken breasts or 4-6 tights

2 garlic cloves, crushed

4-5 lemon slices

1 tbsp capers

1 tbsp dried rosemary

3 tbsp olive oil

salt and pepper, to taste

**Directions:**

Heat olive oil in a skillet over medium-low heat and sauté the garlic for about a minute.

Add the lemon slices to the bottom of the skillet and lay the chicken breasts on top of the lemon. Add in rosemary and capers, season with salt and pepper to taste, cover, and cook, on medium-low, for 20 minutes or until the chicken breasts are cooked through.

Uncover and cook for 2-3 minutes, until the liquid evaporates.

# Chicken and Bacon Frittata

**Serves 4**

**Ingredients:**

1/2 cup chicken, chopped finely

3 oz bacon, chopped

4-5 green onions, finely chopped

5 oz frozen chopped spinach, defrosted and excess moisture squeezed out

1 small tomato, diced

5 eggs whisked

4 tbsp milk

1/2 tsp dried thyme

4 tbsp olive oil

**Directions:**

Heat olive oil in an oven-proof pan and gently cook the chicken until almost cooked through. Add the green onions and tomato and cook for another minute. Add in the spinach and mix well.

In a medium bowl, whisk eggs, milk and thyme. Pour over the top of the meat and vegetable mixture, making sure it covers it well.

Bake in a preheated to 360 F oven for about 15 minutes, or until eggs are cooked through.

# Chicken and Zucchini Frittata

**Serves 4**

**Ingredients:**

1 cup chicken, chopped finely

3 green onions, finely chopped

1 garlic clove, chopped

1 zucchini, peeled and diced

1 tomato, diced

2 tbsp dill, finely chopped

5 eggs

1 cup grated Parmesan cheese

3 tbsp olive oil

*Directions:*

In and oven-proof pan, heat olive oil and gently cook the chicken until almost cooked through. Add in the onion and garlic and cook for another minute, stirring.

Add the zucchini and tomato and cook for for 3-4 minutes, until lightly cooked.

In a medium bowl, whisk eggs, Parmesan cheese and dill together. Pour over the top of the chicken and vegetable mixture, making sure that it covers it well.

Bake in a preheated to 360 F oven for around 15 minutes, until set. Garnish with fresh dill.

# Beef and Pumpkin Stew

**Serves 4-5**

**Ingredients:**

2 lbs lean beef, cubed

2 cups cubed pumpkin

1 small onion, chopped

2 garlic cloves, chopped

1 tomato, diced

zest of one orange

1 bay leaf

1 tsp paprika

4 tbsp olive oil

salt and black pepper, to taste

3 green onions, chopped, to serve

**Directions:**

Heat a stew pot and brown the meat in olive oil.

Add remaining ingredients and sauté for 1-2 minutes.

Add enough water to cover everything, bring to a boil, reduce heat to low, cover, and simmer for 60 minutes, stirring occasionally, until beef is cooked through.

Sprinkle with green onions and serve.

# Beef and Onion Stew

**Serves 6**

**Ingredients:**

2 lbs lean beef, cubed

3 lbs shallots, peeled

5 garlic cloves, peeled, whole

3 tbsp tomato paste

1 bay leaf

4 tbsp olive oil

3 tbsp red wine vinegar

1 tsp salt

**Directions:**

Heat a stew pot and brown the meat in olive oil.

Add in remaining ingredients and enough water to cover everything.

Bring to a boil, reduce heat to low, cover, and simmer for 90 minutes, stirring occasionally, until beef is cooked through.

# Beef Stew with Green Peas

**Serves 6**

**Ingredients:**

2 lbs stewing beef

2 bags(10 oz each) frozen peas

1 onion, chopped

3-4 garlic cloves, cut

2 carrots, chopped

1/3 cup water

1/4 cup olive oil

1 tsp salt

1 tbsp paprika

1/2 cup fresh dill, finely chopped

1 cup yogurt (optional)

**Directions:**

Season the meat pieces with salt and black pepper. Heat olive oil in a large stewing pot and sauté onion and meat until the meat is well browned.

Add in paprika, carrots, garlic, frozen peas and water.

Bring to a boil, reduce heat, cover, and simmer for an hour. Serve sprinkled with fresh dill and a dollop of yogurt.

# Beef and Spinach Stew

**Serves 6**

**Ingredients:**

1 lb stewing beef

10 oz frozen spinach or 6 cups fresh spinach leaves, chopped

1 onion, chopped

1 carrot, chopped

1 cup button white mushrooms, cut

1 tomato, diced

3 garlic cloves, crushed

1 cup beef broth

4 tbsp olive oil

6 oz butter

1 tbsp paprika

salt and pepper, to taste

**Directions:**

In a large stewing pot, heat the butter and olive oil and seal the beef pieces. Add in onion, carrot, mushrooms and garlic and sauté for a few minutes.

Add paprika and beef broth and bring to a boil then reduce heat and simmer, covered, for 40 minutes.

Add in tomato and spinach, season with salt and pepper, stir, and simmer, uncovered, for 5 minutes more.

# Mediterranean Beef Casserole

**Serves 6**

**Ingredients:**

2 lb lean steak, cut into large pieces

3 onions, sliced

4 garlic cloves, cut

2 red peppers, cut

1 green pepper, cut

1 zucchini, peeled and cut

3 tomatoes, quartered

2 tbsp tomato paste or purée

1/2 cup green olives, pitted

1/2 cup dry red wine

1/2 cup of water

1 tsp dried oregano

salt and black pepper, to taste

**Directions:**

Heat olive oil in a deep oven-proof casserole and seal the beef.

Add vegetables and stir to combine.

Dilute the tomato paste in half a cup of water and pour it over the meat mixture together with the wine.

Season with salt and pepper and bake, stirring halfway through, in a preheated to 350 F for one hour.

# Beef and Broccoli Stir Fry

**Serves 4**

**Ingredients:**

1/2 lb flank steak, cut in strips

3 cups broccoli florets

1 onion, chopped

1 cup white button mushrooms, chopped

1 cup beef broth

1/3 cup cashew nuts

2 tbsp soy sauce

1 tbsp honey

1 tsp lemon zest

1 tsp grated ginger

3 tbsp olive oil

1 tsp cornstarch

**Directions:**

Place the meat in the freezer for 20 minutes then cut it in thin slices. Place it in a bowl together with soy sauce, honey, lemon zest and ginger. Stir to coat well and set aside for 30 minutes.

Stir fry steak in olive oil over high heat for 2-3 minutes until cooked through. Add and stir fry broccoli, onion, mushrooms and cashews. Stir in spice. Dilute cornstarch into beef broth and add it to the meat mixture. Stir until thickened.

# Beef Stew with Quince

**Serves 6-8**

**Ingredients:**

2 lbs chuck roast, cut into 2 inch pieces

2 onions, chopped

2-3 tomatoes, pureed

1-2 bay leaves

1 cinnamon stick

1 cup dry white wine

3 quinces, peeled, cored and cubed

5-6 prunes

1 tsp paprika

1 tsp salt

1/2 tsp black pepper

1 tbsp honey

6 tbsp olive oil

**Directions:**

Heat olive oil in a large pot over medium-high heat. Seal the meat then add and sauté the onions for 6-8 minutes.

Add in the wine, bay leaves, cinnamon, tomato puree, salt, pepper, and enough water to cover the meat. Stir to combine and bring the pot to a simmer.

Add the quince to the stew pot along with the prunes and honey. Stir, cover, and simmer for two hours over low heat.

Stir occasionally and make sure there is enough liquid in the pot.

If it looks dry, add some water.

Before serving discard the bay leaves and the cinnamon stick.

# Spanish Beef Stew

**Serves 6-8**

**Ingredients:**

2 lbs stewing beef

1 tbsp flour

1 cup beef broth

1/2 cup dry red wine

3 leeks, chopped

6 garlic cloves, halved

2 onions, chopped

1 carrot, sliced

1 celery rib, chopped

1 tomato, chopped

2 oz cooking chocolate

1/4 tsp cinnamon

1/4 cup olive oil

**Directions:**

Heat the olive oil in a large pot. Seal the stewing meat for 3-4 minutes, or until well browned on all sides. Add in the flour and stir. Add the wine and cook for 2-3 minutes, stirring.

Add the garlic, onions, tomatoes, carrot, celery and leaks to the pot and stir to combine. Add chocolate and beef broth, stir, and bring to a boil.

Reduce heat, cover partially and simmer for an hour and a half or until the meat is cooked through.

# Ground Beef and Chickpea Casserole

**Serves 6**

**Ingredients:**

1 lb ground beef

1 onion, chopped

2 garlic cloves, crushed

1 can chickpeas, drained

1 can sweet corn, drained

1 can tomato sauce

1/2 cup water

2 bay leaves

1 tsp dried oregano

1/2 tsp salt

1/2 tsp cumin

3 tbsp olive oil

black pepper, to taste

**Directions:**

Heat olive oil in a casserole over medium-high heat. Add in the onion and sauté for 4-5 minutes. Add garlic and sauté for 1-2 minutes more. Add in the ground beef and cook for 5 minutes, stirring, until browned. Stir in cumin and bay leaves, tomatoes, corn and chickpeas.

Bake in a preheated to 350 F for 20 minutes, or until the beef is cooked through. Remove the bay leaves and serve over rice pilaf or couscous.

# Spinach with Ground Beef

**Serves 4**

**Ingredients:**

10 oz ground beef

6 cups fresh spinach, chopped

1 tomato, cubed

1 onion, finely chopped

1/3 cup rice

4 tbsp olive oil

1 tsp paprika

salt, to taste

black pepper, to taste

**Directions:**

Heat olive oil in a large pot and sauté the onion for about 2-3 minutes. Add in ground beef, paprika, salt and black pepper and stir to combine.

Cook until the ground beef turns brown. Stir in rice, the diced tomato and simmer, covered, for 20 minutes.

Add spinach and cook until it wilts. Serve with a dollop of yogurt.

# Delicious One-Pot Ground Beef Pasta

**Serves 4**

**Ingredients:**

8 oz dry pasta

1 lb ground beef

3 cups hot water

1/2 onion, finely cut

4-5 white button mushrooms, chopped

2 garlic cloves, chopped

6-7 gherkins, finely chopped

1/2 cup sweet corn

1 cup parsley, finely cut

1/2 cup heavy cream

3 tbsp olive oil

salt and black pepper, to taste

**Directions:**

Heat olive oil in deep saucepan and sauté the onion for about 2-3 minutes. Add in ground beef and sauté for 3-4 minutes or until the beef turns brown.

Add in hot water, pasta, mushrooms, garlic, gherkins, sweet corn and parsley and simmer for 10 minutes.

Add in the cream, salt and pepper to taste and Parmesan cheese. Stir and simmer for 1-2 minutes more. Remove from heat and set aside for a few minutes.

Taste to adjust seasonings and serve.

# Sausage and Beans

**Serves 4**

**Ingredients:**

1.7 lb lean beef sausages

1 big onion, thinly sliced

2 garlic cloves, crushed

2 cups canned white beans, drained, rinsed

1 cup canned tomatoes, drained, diced

1 tsp paprika

1 tbsp dried mint

1 tbsp sunflower oil

1/2 cup finely cut parsley, to serve

**Directions:**

Heat a large non-stick frying pan over medium heat. Cook sausages for 8 to 10 minutes or until browned.

Add in onions, garlic and paprika and sauté gently for 3-4 minutes or until onion is soft. Add beans, tomatoes and mint. Stir, and simmer for 15 minutes or until sauce is thick.

Serve into bowls sprinkled with fresh parsley.

# Mediterranean Pork Casserole

**Serves 4**

**Ingredients:**

1 1/2 lb pork loin, cut into cubes

1 large onion, chopped

1 cup white button mushrooms, cut

2 garlic cloves, finely chopped

1 green pepper, deseeded and cut into strips

1 red pepper, deseeded and cut into strips

2 tomatoes, chopped

½ cup chicken broth

2 tbsp olive oil

1 tsp summer savory

1 tsp paprika

salt and black pepper, to taste

**Directions:**

Add the olive oil to a casserole dish and seal the pork cubes for about 5 minutes, stirring continuously. Lower the heat, add the onion and garlic and sauté for 3-4 minutes until the onion is soft.

Stir in paprika and savory and season with salt and black pepper to taste. Add in peppers, tomatoes, chicken broth and mushrooms. Cover with a lid or aluminum foil and bake for 1 hour at 350 F, or until the pork is tender.

Uncover and bake for 5 minutes more. Serve with mashed potatoes or rice pilaf.

# Pork and Rice Casserole

**Serves 5-6**

**Ingredients:**

1.5 lb pork, cubed (leg or neck)

1 onion, chopped

2 cups rice, washed

5 cups water

4 tbsp olive oil

1/2 cup finely cut parsley leaves, to serve

**Directions:**

Heat oil in a large oven-proof casserole dish on medium-high heat. Cook pork, turning, for 4-5 minutes, or until browned.

Add rice and cook for 2-3 minutes, stirring continuously, until transparent. Add 5 cups of warm water, stir well, and bake in a preheated to 350 F oven for 40 minutes, stirring halfway through.

When ready, sprinkle with parsley, set aside for 2-3 minutes and serve.

# Pork Roast and Cabbage

**Serves 4**

**Ingredients:**

2 cups cooked pork roast, chopped

1/2 head cabbage

1 onion, chopped

1 lemon, juice only

1 tomato, chopped

2 tbsp olive oil

1 tsp paprika

1/2 tsp cumin

black pepper, to taste

**Directions:**

In an oven-proof casserole dish, heat olive oil and gently sauté cabbage, pork and onions. Add in cumin, paprika, lemon juice, tomato and stir.

Cover and bake at 350 F for 20-25 minutes, or until vegetables are tender.

# Orange Pork Chops

**Serves 4**

**Ingredients:**

4 pork chops, about 4 oz each

1 onion, thinly sliced

4 garlic cloves, crushed

3 tbsp olive oil

1/4 tsp cumin

1/2 tsp dried oregano

1 tsp black pepper

1 tbsp raw honey

1 cup orange juice

**Directions:**

Crush the garlic, oregano, black pepper and cumin together into a paste. Rub each chop with the garlic paste and arrange them in a casserole dish.

Dilute one tablespoon of honey into the orange juice and pour it over the chops. Add in onions, stir, and bake in a preheated to 350 F on for 30 minutes, or until the chops are cooked through.

# Pork and Mushroom Crock Pot

**Serves 4**

**Ingredients:**

2 lbs pork tenderloin, sliced

2 cups chopped white button mushrooms

1 can cream of mushroom soup

½ cup sour cream

4 tbsp chopped tarragon

1/2 tsp black pepper

1/2 tsp salt

**Directions:**

Spray the slow cooker with non stick spray.

Combine all ingredients into the slow cooker. Cover, and cook on low for 7-9 hours.

# Bacon and Mushroom Frittata

**Serves 4**

**Ingredients:**

6-7 oz bacon, chopped

1 cup white button mushrooms, chopped

½ onion, chopped

1 garlic clove, chopped

1 tomato, thinly sliced

1/2 tsp black pepper

1 tsp dried parsley

5 eggs, whisked

3 tbsp milk

1 tbsp olive oil

**Directions:**

In and oven-proof pan, heat olive oil and gently cook the bacon until almost cooked through. Add in the onion and garlic and cook for another minute, stirring. Add the mushrooms, stir, and cook on medium-high heat for 3-4 minutes.

In a medium bowl, whisk eggs, milk, salt, black pepper and parsley together. Pour over the top of the bacon and mushroom mixture, making sure that it covers it well.

Lay the tomato slices on top and bake in a preheated to 360 F oven for around 15 minutes, until set.

## Brussels Sprouts with Bacon and Onion

**Serves 6**

**Ingredients:**

4 strips bacon, cut

2 tbsp olive oil

2 lb Brussels sprouts, halved

1 large onion, chopped

1/2 cup sour cream

salt and freshly ground black pepper, to taste

**Directions:**

In an oven-proof casserole, cook bacon over medium-high heat until crispy.

Add in onions and Brussels sprouts and bake, in a preheated to 350 F oven, stirring occasionally, until sprouts are golden brown.

Stir in sour cream, sprinkle with Parmesan cheese and bake for 5 more minutes.

# Zucchini Bake

**Serves 4**

**Ingredients:**

5 medium zucchinis, peeled and grated

1 carrot, grated

1 small tomato, diced

1 onion, halved, thinly sliced

2 garlic cloves, crushed

1 cup self-raising flour, sifted

5 eggs, lightly whisked

1/3 cup sunflower oil

1/2 cup fresh dill, finely cut

1 cup grated feta cheese

2 cups yogurt, to serve (optional)

**Directions:**

Combine zucchinis, carrot, tomato, onion, garlic, and dill in a bowl. Add flour, eggs, oil and cheese. Season and stir to combine.

Transfer the zucchini mixture into a greased casserole dish and bake for 20-30 minutes in a preheated to 350 F oven. Serve with yogurt.

# Baked Cauliflower

**Serves 4**

**Ingredients:**

1 medium cauliflower, cut into florets

4 garlic cloves, lightly crushed

4-5 fresh rosemary leaves, finely cut

salt, to taste

black pepper, to taste

1/4 cup olive oil

1/2 cup sour cream

1/2 cup grated Parmesan Cheese

**Directions:**

In a bowl, mix oil, rosemary, salt, pepper and garlic together. Add in cauliflower florets and toss to combine.

Place in a casserole dish in one layer. Roast in a preheated oven at 350 F for 20 minutes.

Stir in sour cream, sprinkle with Parmesan cheese and bake for 10 more minutes.

# Potato and Zucchini Bake

**Serves 6**

**Ingredients:**

1½ lb potatoes, peeled and sliced into rounds

5 zucchinis, peeled and sliced into rounds

2 onions, sliced

3 tomatoes, pureed

½ cup water

4 tbsp olive oil

1 tsp dried oregano

1/3 cup fresh parsley leaves, chopped

salt and black pepper, to taste

**Directions:**

Place potatoes, zucchinis and onions in a large, shallow oven-proof baking dish. Pour over the olive oil and pureed tomatoes. Add salt and freshly ground pepper to taste and toss the everything together. Add in water.

Bake in a preheated to 350 F oven for 45 minutes, stirring halfway through.

## Artichoke and Onion Frittata

**Serves 4**

**Ingredients:**

1 small onion, chopped

1 cup marinated artichoke hearts, drained

6 eggs

1 garlic clove, crushed

1 tbsp olive oil

salt and freshly ground black pepper

1/2 cup fresh parsley, finely cut, to serve

**Directions:**

Heat oil in a non-stick oven pan over medium heat and sauté onion stirring occasionally, for 5-6 minutes or until golden brown. Add artichokes and cook for 2 minutes or until heated through.

Whisk eggs with garlic until combined well. Season with salt and pepper. Pour the egg mixture over the artichoke mixture.

Reduce heat, cover, and cook for 10 minutes or until the frittata is set around the edge but still runny in the center. Place pan into preheated oven and cook 4-5 until golden brown.

Remove from oven and cut into wedges. Serve sprinkled with parsley.

# Green Pea and Mushroom Stew

**Serves 4**

**Ingredients:**

1 cup green peas (fresh or frozen)

5 large white button mushrooms, sliced

3 green onions, chopped

1 big carrot, chopped

1-2 cloves garlic

4 tbsp sunflower oil

1/2 cup water

1/2 cup finely chopped dill

salt and black pepper, to taste

**Directions:**

In a saucepan, sauté mushrooms, carrot, green onions and garlic. Add in green peas and simmer for 10 minutes until tender.

When ready, sprinkle with dill, and serve.

# Tomato and Leek Stew

**Serves 5-6**

**Ingredients:**

1 lb leeks, cut into rings

1/2 cup vegetable broth

2 tbsp tomato paste

4 tbsp sunflower oil

1 tbsp dried mint

salt to taste

fresh ground pepper to taste

**Directions:**

Heat oil in a heavy wide saucepan or sauté pan. Add in leeks, salt, pepper, and sauté, stirring, for 5 minutes.

Add in vegetable broth and bring to a boil.

Cover, and simmer over low heat, stirring often, for about 10-15 minutes or until leeks are tender. Gently stir in tomato paste and dried mint, raise heat to medium, uncover, and simmer for 5 more minutes.

# Potato and Leek Stew

**Serves 4**

**Ingredients:**

12 oz potatoes, diced

2-3 leeks cut into thick rings

5-6 tbsp olive oil

1 cup water

1/2 cup finely cut parsley

1 tsp paprika

salt and black pepper, to taste

**Directions:**

Heat olive oil in a heavy wide saucepan or sauté pan. Add in leeks, paprika, salt and pepper, and sauté for 2-3 minutes, stirring.

Add in potatoes and water. The water should cover the vegetables. Bring to a boil and simmer until vegetables are tender.

Sprinkle with finely chopped parsley and serve.

# Baked Bean and Rice Casserole

**Serves 4**

**Ingredients**

1 15 oz can white or red beans, drained

1/2 cup rice

1 cup water

1 onion, chopped

½ bunch parsley, finely cut

1 tbsp dried mint

3 tbsp olive oil

1 tbsp paprika

½ tsp black pepper

1 tsp salt

**Directions:**

Heat olive oil in a deep oven-proof casserole and gently sauté the chopped onion. Add in paprika and rice and cook, stirring, for a minute.

Add in water or vegetable broth and beans. Season with salt and black pepper, stir in mint and parsley, and bake in a preheated to 350 F oven for 20 minutes.

# Creamy Green Pea and Rice Casserole

**Serves 4**

**Ingredients**

1 onion, very finely cut

1 bag frozen peas

2-3 garlic cloves, chopped

3-4 mushrooms, chopped

1/2 cup white rice

1 cup water

4 tbsp olive oil

1/2 cup sour cream

2/3 cup grated Parmesan cheese

1/2 cup fresh dill, finely cut

salt and black pepper, to taste

**Directions:**

In a deep oven-proof casserole dish, heat olive oil and sauté the onions, garlic and mushrooms for 2-3 minutes. Add in rice and cook, stirring, for 1 minute. Add in a cup of warm water, the frozen peas, and the dill.

Stir to combine and bake in a preheated to 350 F oven, for 20 minutes.

Stir in sour cream, sprinkle with Parmesan cheese, bake for 2-3 more minutes, and serve.

## Zucchini and Rice Stew

**Serves 4**

**Ingredients:**

2 lbs zucchinis, diced

1 cup green onions, finely chopped

5 tbsp sunflower oil

2 cups water

2 tomatoes, diced

1 tsp salt

1 tsp paprika

salt and black pepper, to taste

2½ cups water

1 cup chopped fresh dill

**Directions:**

Gently sauté green onions in oil and a little water.

Transfer onions in a baking dish, add in zucchinis, tomatoes, rice, salt, paprika, pepper and water.

Stir to combine, cover with a lid or foil and bake in preheated to 350 F oven for 30 minutes, or until rice is done. Sprinkle with dill.

# Spinach with Rice

**Serves 4**

**Ingredients:**

1.5 lb fresh spinach, washed, drained and chopped

1/2 cup rice

1 onion, chopped

1 carrot, chopped

5 tbsp olive oil

2 cups water

**Directions:**

Heat oil in a large skillet and cook the onions and the carrot until soft. Add in paprika and rice and stir.

Add two cups of warm water stirring constantly as the rice absorbs it, and simmer for 10 minutes.

Wash the spinach cut it in strips then add to the rice and cook until it wilts. Remove from heat and season to taste.

# Eggplant Casserole

**Serves 4**

**Ingredients:**

2 medium eggplants, peeled and diced

1 cup canned tomatoes, drained and diced

1 zucchini, peeled and diced

9-10 black olives, pitted

1 onion, chopped

4 garlic cloves, chopped

2 tbsp tomato paste

1 cup canned tomatoes, drained and diced

3 tbsp olive oil

1 tbsp paprika

salt and black pepper, to taste

1 cup parsley, chopped, to serve

**Directions:**

Heat olive oil in a deep casserole dish and gently sauté onions, garlic, and eggplants. Add in paprika and tomato paste and sauté, stirring, for 1-2 minutes. Add in the rest of the ingredients.

Cover, and bake at 350 F for 30-40 minutes. Sprinkle with parsley and serve.

# Eggplant and Chickpea Casserole

**Serves 4**

**Ingredients:**

2-3 eggplants, peeled and diced

1 onion, chopped

2-3 garlic cloves, crushed

1 can chickpeas, (15 oz), drained

1 can tomatoes, (15 oz), undrained, diced

1 tsp paprika

½ tsp cinnamon

1 tsp cumin

4 tbsp olive oil

salt and pepper, to taste

1 cup grated Parmesan cheese

**Directions:**

Peel and dice the eggplants. Heat olive oil in a deep oven-proof casserole and sauté the onions and crushed garlic.

Add in paprika, cumin and cinnamon. Stir well to coat evenly. Sauté for 3-4 minutes until the onions have softened.

Add the eggplant, tomatoes and chickpeas. Bake in a preheated to 350 F oven, covered, for 15 minutes, or until the eggplant is tender.

Uncover and sprinkle with Parmesan cheese. Bake for a few more minutes until the liquid evaporates and the cheese is golden.

# Ratatouille

**Serves 4**

**Ingredients:**

1 eggplant, cut into small cubes

2 large tomatoes, chopped

2 zucchinis, sliced

1 onion, sliced into rings

1 green pepper, sliced

6-7 sliced white button mushrooms

3 cloves garlic, crushed

2 tsp dried parsley

½ cup Parmesan cheese

3 tbsp olive oil

**Directions:**

Place eggplant pieces on a tray and sprinkle with plenty of salt. Let sit for 30 minutes, then rinse with cold water.

Heat olive oil in an oven-proof casserole over medium heat. Gently sauté garlic for a minute or two. Add in parsley and eggplant. Continue sautéing until eggplant is soft. Sprinkle with a tablespoon of Parmesan cheese. Spread zucchinis in an even layer over the eggplant. Sprinkle with a little more cheese.

Continue layering onion, mushrooms, pepper and tomatoes, covering each layer with a sprinkling of Parmesan cheese.

Bake in a preheated to 350 F oven for 40 minutes.

# Rice Stuffed Bell Peppers

**Serves 4-5**

**Ingredients:**

8 bell peppers, cored and seeded

1 1/2 cups rice

2 onions, chopped

1 tomato, chopped

1/2 cup fresh parsley, chopped

3 tbsp olive oil

1 tbsp paprika

**Directions:**

Heat the olive oil and sauté the onions for 2-3 minutes. Add in paprika, rice, diced tomato and season with salt and pepper. Add ½ cup of hot water and cook the rice, stirring, until the water is absorbed.

Stuff each pepper with rice mixture using a spoon. Every pepper should be ¾ full. Arrange the peppers in a deep oven-proof dish and top up with warm water to half fill the dish.

Cover and bake for about 20 minutes at 350 F. Uncover and cook for another 15 minutes until the peppers are well cooked through.

# Green Bean and Potato Stew

**Serves 5-6**

**Ingredients:**

2 cups green beans, fresh or frozen

2 onions, chopped

3-4 potatoes, peeled and diced

2 carrots, cut

4 cloves garlic, crushed

1 cup fresh parsley, chopped

1/2 cup fresh dill, finely chopped

4 tbsp olive oil

1/2 cup water

2 tsp tomato paste

salt and pepper, to taste

**Directions:**

Heat olive oil in a deep saucepan and gently sauté the onions and garlic. Add in green beans and the remaining ingredients.

Cover and simmer over medium heat for about an hour or until all vegetables are tender.

Check after 30 minutes; add more water if necessary. Serve sprinkled with fresh dill.

# Cabbage and Rice Stew

**Serves 4**

**Ingredients:**

1 cup long grain white rice

2 cups water

2 tbsp olive oil

1 small onion, chopped

1 clove garlic, crushed

1/4 head cabbage, cored and shredded

2 tomatoes, diced

1 tbsp paprika

1/2 cup parsley, finely cut

salt and black pepper, to taste

**Directions:**

Heat the olive oil in a large pot. Add in onion and garlic and cook until transparent. Add paprika, rice and water, stir, and bring to boil.

Simmer for 10 minutes. Add in cabbage, tomatoes, and cook for about 20 minutes, stirring occasionally, until the cabbage cooks down. Season with salt and pepper and serve sprinkled with parsley.

# Rice with Leeks and Olives

**Serves 4-6**

**Ingredients:**

6 large leeks, cleaned and sliced into bite sized pieces (about 6-7 cups of sliced leeks)

1 large onion, cut

20 black olives pitted, chopped

1/2 cup hot water

1/4 cup olive oil

1 cup rice

2 cups boiling water

black pepper, to taste

**Directions:**

In a large saucepan, sauté the leeks and onion in olive oil for 4-5 minutes. Cut and add the olives and 1/2 cup of water. Bring temperature down, cover saucepan, and cook for 5 minutes, stirring occasionally.

Add in rice and 2 cups of hot water, bring to a boil, cover, and simmer for 15 more minutes, stirring occasionally.

Remove from heat and allow to 'sit' for 30 minutes before serving so that the rice can absorb any liquid left.

# Rice and Tomato Stew

**Serves 6-7**

**Ingredients:**

1 cup rice

1 big onion, chopped

2 cups canned tomatoes, diced or 5 big ripe tomatoes

1 tbsp paprika

1/4 cup olive oil

1 tsp summer savory

½ cup fresh parsley, finely cut

1 tsp sugar

**Directions:**

Wash and drain the rice. In a large saucepan, sauté the onion in olive oil for 4-5 minutes. Add in paprika and rice, stirring constantly, until the rice becomes transparent.

Stir in 2 cups of hot water and the tomatoes. Mix well and season with salt, pepper, savory and a tsp of sugar to neutralize the acidic taste of the tomatoes.

Simmer over medium heath for about 20 minutes. When ready sprinkle with parsley.

## Okra and Tomato Casserole

**Serves 4-5**

**Ingredients:**

1 lb okra, stem ends trimmed

4 large tomatoes, cut into wedges

3 garlic cloves, chopped

3 tbsp olive oil

1 tsp salt

black pepper, to taste

**Directions:**

In a large casserole, mix together trimmed okra, sliced tomatoes, olive oil and chopped garlic. Add salt and pepper and toss to combine.

Bake in a preheated to 350 F oven for 45 minutes, or until the okra is tender.

# Spinach with Eggs

**Serves 2**

**Ingredients:**

1 lb spinach, fresh or frozen

1 onion, finely cut

4 eggs

3 tbsp olive oil

1/4 tsp cumin

1 tsp paprika

salt and pepper, to taste

*Directions:*

Heat olive oil on medium-low heat in a skillet. Gently sauté onion for 3-4 minutes. Add paprika and cumin and stir to combine.

Add spinach and sauté some more until it wilts. Season with salt and black pepper to taste.

Prepare 4 holes on the spinach bed for the eggs. Break an egg into each hole.

Cover and cook until eggs are cooked through. Serve with bread and a dollop of yogurt.

# Mish-Mash

**Serves 5-6**

**Ingredients:**

1 onion, chopped

1 green bell pepper, chopped

1 red bell peppers chopped

4 tomatoes, cubed

8-9 eggs

9 oz feta cheese, crumbled

3 tbsp olive oil

1/2 cup parsley, finely cut

salt and black pepper, to taste

**Directions:**

In a large pan sauté onions over medium heat, till transparent. Reduce heat and add bell peppers and garlic. Continue cooking until soft. Add the tomatoes and continue simmering until the mixture is almost dry.

Add the cheese and all eggs and cook until well mixed and not too liquid. Season with black pepper and remove from heat.

Sprinkle with parsley and serve.

# Vegetable Quinoa Pilaf

**Serves 6**

**Ingredients:**

1 cup quinoa

2 cups water

1 red bell pepper, chopped

1 small eggplant, chopped

1 zucchini, chopped

1/2 onion, thinly sliced

2 garlic cloves, cut

1 tsp summer savory

1 tsp dried oregano

3 tbsp olive oil

salt and pepper, to taste

**Directions:**

Rinse quinoa very well in a fine mesh strainer under running water; set aside to drain.

Heat olive oil in a heavy based saucepan over medium-high heat. Add the bell pepper, eggplant, onion, garlic and zucchini. Sauté, stirring, for 2 minutes then add in the spice, salt and black pepper, water and quinoa and bring to a boil.

Lower heat, cover, and simmer for 15 minutes.

## Spinach, Lentil and Quinoa Casserole

*Serves 6*

*Ingredients:*

½ cup brown lentils

½ cup quinoa

3 cups fresh spinach or about half package of frozen spinach, thawed

1 onion, chopped

2 medium carrots, chopped

2 cloves garlic, cut

3 tbsp olive oil

1 tbsp paprika

2 tsp summer savory

2 cups water

salt and black pepper, to taste

**Directions:**

Heath the olive oil in a deep casserole dish and gently sauté the onion and carrots for 4-5 minutes. Add in garlic, paprika, savory and lentils and sauté for a minute more while stirring. Stir in the water and bake at 350 F for 15 minutes.

Wash and rinse the quinoa and add it to the casserole with salt and pepper to taste. Stir well and bake for another 10 minutes. Cut the spinach and add it to casserole dish.

Bake for 4-5 more minutes and serve.

# Rich Vegetable One-Pot Pasta

**Serves 4**

**Ingredients:**

12 oz dry pasta

11/2 cup tomato sauce

2 cups water

1/2 onion, finely chopped

1 cup white button mushrooms, chopped

1/3 cup black olives, pitted

1/2 small eggplant, peeled and cubed

1 red pepper, cut

3 tbsp olive oil

1 tsp dried basil

1 tsp black pepper

1 tsp salt

1/2 cup parsley, finely cut

**Directions:**

In a large saucepan, heat olive oil over medium-high heat. Gently sauté the finely chopped onion and red pepper for 1-2 minutes. Add in the mushrooms and eggplant and sauté for a few minutes more, stirring.

Add the tomato sauce, water, salt, pepper, basil and black olives and bring to a boil. Add in pasta, cover, and simmer for about 10 minutes or until the pasta is cooked to al dente.

Taste to adjust seasonings, sprinkle with parsley and serve.

# One-Pot Broccoli Pasta

**Serves 4**

**Ingredients:**

8 oz dry pasta

1.5 lb broccoli, cut into florets

4 cups water

1/2 onion, finely chopped

4-5 white button mushrooms, chopped

2 garlic cloves, chopped

1/2 cup frozen peas

1/2 cup sweet corn

1/4 cup heavy cream

3 tbsp olive oil

1 tsp dried basil

salt and black pepper, to taste

a handful of baby rocket leaves, to serve

**Directions:**

Add water, pasta, broccoli, mushrooms, garlic, onion, peas and sweet corn to a large pot, set over high heat, and bring to a boil. Lower heat and simmer for 10 minutes, stirring constantly.

Add in the cream, salt and pepper to taste and simmer for 1-2 minutes more. Remove from heat and set aside for a few minutes.

Taste to adjust seasonings, sprinkle with baby rocket leaves, and serve.

# FREE BONUS RECIPES: 10 Ridiculously Easy Jam and Jelly Recipes Anyone Can Make

# A Different Strawberry Jam

**Makes 6-7 11 oz jars**

**Ingredients:**

4 lb fresh small strawberries (stemmed and cleaned)

5 cups sugar

1 cup water

2 tbsp lemon juice or 1 tsp citric acid

**Directions:**

Mix water and sugar and bring to the boil. Simmer sugar syrup for 5-6 minutes then slowly drop in the cleaned strawberries. Stir and bring to the boil again.

Lower heat and simmer, stirring and skimming any foam off the top once or twice. Drop a small amount of the jam on a plate and wait a minute to see if it has thickened. If it has gelled enough, turn off the heat. If not, keep boiling and test every 5 minutes until ready. Two or three minutes before you remove the jam from the heat, add lemon juice or citric acid and stir well.

Ladle the hot jam in the jars until 1/8-inch from the top. Place the lid on top and flip the jar upside down. Continue until all of the jars are filled and upside down. Allow the jam to cool completely before turning right-side up. Press on the lid to check and see if it has sealed. If one of the jars lids doesn't pop up- the jar is not sealed–store it in a refrigerator.

# Raspberry Jam

**Makes 4-5 11 oz jars**

**Ingredients:**

4 cups raspberries

4 cups sugar

1 tsp vanilla extract

1/2 tsp citric acid

**Directions:**

Gently wash and drain the raspberries. Lightly crush them with a potato masher, food mill or a food processor. Do not puree, it is better to have bits of fruit. Sieve half of the raspberry pulp to remove some of the seeds.

Combine sugar and raspberries in a wide, thick-bottomed pot and bring mixture to a full rolling boil, stirring constantly. Skim any scum or foam that rises to the surface. Boil until the jam sets.

Test by putting a small drop on a cold plate – if the jam is set, it will wrinkle when given a small poke with your finger. Add citric acid, vanilla, and stir. Simmer for 2-3 minutes more, then ladle into hot jars. Flip upside down or process 10 minutes in boiling water.

# Raspberry-Peach Jam

**Makes 4-5 11 oz jars**

**Ingredients:**

2 lb peaches

1 1/2 cup raspberries

4 cups sugar

1 tsp citric acid

**Directions:**

Wash and slice the peaches. Clean the raspberries and combine them with the peaches is a wide, heavy-bottomed saucepan. Cover with sugar and set aside for a few hours or overnight.

Bring the fruit and sugar to a boil over medium heat, stirring occasionally. Remove any foam that rises to the surface.

Boil until the jam sets. Add citric acid and stir. Simmer for 2-3 minutes more, then ladle into hot jars. Flip upside down or process 10 minutes in boiling water.

# Blueberry Jam

**Makes 4-5 11 oz jars**

**Ingredients:**

4 cups granulated sugar

3 cups blueberries (frozen and thawed or fresh)

3/4 cup honey

2 tbsp lemon juice

1 tsp lemon zest

**Directions:**

Gently wash and drain the blueberries. Lightly crush them with a potato masher, food mill or a food processor. Add the honey, lemon juice, and lemon zest, then bring to a boil over medium-high heat. Boil for 10-15 minutes, stirring from time to time. Boil until the jam sets.

Test by putting a small drop on a cold plate – if the jam is set, it will wrinkle when given a small poke with your finger. Skim off any foam, then ladle the jam into jars. Seal, flip upside down or process for 10 minutes in boiling water.

# Triple Berry Jam

**Makes 4-5 11 oz jars**

**Ingredients:**

1 cup strawberries

1 cup raspberries

2 cups blueberries

4 cups sugar

1 tsp citric acid

**Directions:**

Mix berries and add sugar. Set aside for a few hours or overnight. Bring the fruit and sugar to the boil over medium heat, stirring frequently. Remove any foam that rises to the surface. Boil until the jam sets. Add citric acid, salt and stir.

Simmer for 2-3 minutes more, then ladle into hot jars. Flip upside down or process 10 minutes in boiling water.

# Red Currant Jelly

**Makes 6-7 11 oz jars**

**Ingredients:**

2 lb fresh red currants

1/2 cup water

3 cups sugar

1 tsp citric acid

**Directions:**

Place the currants into a large pot, and crush with a potato masher or berry crusher. Add in water, and bring to a boil. Simmer for 10 minutes. Strain the fruit through a jelly or cheese cloth and measure out 4 cups of the juice. Pour the juice into a large saucepan, and stir in the sugar.

Bring to full rolling boil, then simmer for 20-30 minutes, removing any foam that may rise to the surface. When the jelly sets, ladle in hot jars, flip upside down or process in boiling water for 10 minutes.

# White Cherry Jam

**Makes 3-4 11 oz jars**

**Ingredients:**

2 lb cherries

3 cups sugar

2 cups water

1 tsp citric acid

**Directions:**

Wash and stone cherries. Combine water and sugar and bring to the boil. Boil for 5-6 minutes then remove from heat and add cherries. Bring to a rolling boil and cook until set. Add citric acid, stir and boil 1-2 minutes more.

Ladle in hot jars, flip upside down or process in boiling water for 10 minutes.

# Cherry Jam

**Makes 3-4 11 oz jars**

**Ingredients:**

2 lb fresh cherries, pitted, halved

4 cups sugar

1/2 cup lemon juice

**Directions:**

Place the cherries in a large saucepan. Add sugar and set aside for an hour. Add the lemon juice and place over low heat. Cook, stirring occasionally, for 10 minutes or until sugar dissolves. Increase heat to high and bring to a rolling boil.

Cook for 5-6 minutes or until jam is set. Remove from heat and ladle hot jam into jars, seal and flip upside down.

# Oven Baked Ripe Fig Jam

**Makes 3-4 11 oz jars**

**Ingredients:**

2 lb ripe figs

2 cups sugar

1 ½ cups water

2 tbsp lemon juice

**Directions:**

Arrange the figs in a Dutch oven, if they are very big, cut them in halves. Add sugar and water and stir well. Bake at 350 F for about one and a half hours. Do not stir.

You can check the readiness by dropping a drop of the syrup in a cup of cold water – if it falls to the bottom without dissolving, the jam is ready. If the drop dissolves before falling, you can bake it a little longer.

Take out of the oven, add lemon juice and ladle in the warm jars. Place the lids on top and flip the jars upside down. Allow the jam to cool completely before turning right-side up.

If you want to process the jams - place them into a large pot, cover the jars with water by at least 2 inches and bring to a boil. Boil for 10 minutes, remove the jars and sit to cool.

# Quince Jam

**Makes 5-6 11 oz jars**

**Ingredients:**

4 lb quinces

5 cups sugar

2 cups water

1 tsp lemon zest

3 tbsp lemon juice

**Directions:**

Combine water and sugar in a deep, thick-bottomed saucepan and bring it to the boil. Simmer, stirring until the sugar has completely dissolved. Rinse the quinces, cut in half, and discard the cores. Grate the quinces, using a cheese grater or a blender to make it faster. Quince flesh tends to darken very quickly, so it is good to do this as fast as possible.

Add the grated quinces to the sugar syrup and cook uncovered, stirring occasionally until the jam turns pink and thickens to desired consistency, about 40 minutes. Drop a small amount of the jam on a plate and wait a minute to see if it has thickened. If it has gelled enough, turn off the heat. If not, keep boiling and test every 2-3 minutes until ready.

Two or three minutes before you remove the jam from the heat, add lemon juice and lemon zest and stir well. Ladle in hot, sterilized jars and flip upside down.

## About the Author

Vesela lives in Bulgaria with her family of six (including the Jack Russell Terrier). Her passion is going green in everyday life and she loves to prepare homemade cosmetic and beauty products for all her family and friends.

Vesela has been publishing her cookbooks for over a year now. If you want to see other healthy family recipes that she has published, together with some natural beauty books, you can check out her Author Page on Amazon.

Printed in Great Britain
by Amazon